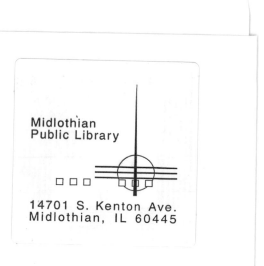

"*And when we allow freedom to ring, when we let it ring from every village and hamlet, from every state and city, we will be able to speed up that day when all of God's children — black men and white men, Jews and Gentiles, Catholics and Protestants — will be able to join hands and to sing in the words of the old Negro spiritual, 'Free at last, free at last; thank God Almighty, we are free at last.'*"

—MARTIN LUTHER KING, JR.

THE MARCH ON WASHINGTON

BY L. S. SUMMER

GRAPHIC DESIGN
Robert E. Bonaker / Graphic Design & Consulting Co.

PROJECT COORDINATOR
James R. Rothaus / James R. Rothaus & Associates

EDITORIAL DIRECTION
Elizabeth Sirimarco Budd

COVER PHOTO
Martin Luther King, Jr., speaking at the Lincoln Memorial
©Bettmann/CORBIS

Library of Congress Cataloging-in-Publication Data
Summer, L. S., 1959–
The march on Washington / by L. S. Summer.
p. cm.
Summary: Explains what events led Martin Luther King, Jr., to
develop his famous speech, "I Have a Dream."
ISBN 1-56766-718-X (lib bdg. : alk. paper)

1.King, Martin Luther, Jr., 1929–1968. I have a dream —
Juvenile literature. 2. Afro-Americans — Civil rights —
Juvenile literature. 3. Civil rights movements — United States
— History — 20th century — Juvenile literature. 4. United
States — Race relations — Juvenile literature. [1. King,
Martin Luther, Jr., 1929–1968. 2. Afro-Americans — Civil
rights. 3. Civil rights movements.] I. Title

E185.97.K5 A5 2000
323'.092 — dc21   99-047446

Contents

The Greatest Demonstration for Freedom

Wednesday, August 28, 1963, was a beautiful summer day. The afternoon sun shone on the Lincoln Memorial. More than 250,000 people gathered on the lawn below. Most of these people were African Americans. Another 60,000 white people joined them. Some were rich celebrities. Some were poor laborers. There were people from many different religions. People from all parts of the United States came to Washington, D.C., that day. They came to march for freedom. They came to demand justice.

This event was called the March on Washington for Jobs and Freedom. People of all races, religions, and incomes worked together to make it happen. It was shown on television around the world. The world watched these Americans in action.

The high point of the day was a speech by the Reverend Dr. Martin Luther King. Dr. King was an important black leader. He spoke out about the difficult lives of African Americans. In 1865, nearly 100 years before the march, slavery became illegal in the United States. Then the U.S. Congress passed the 14th Amendment in 1868. This act, along with the 15th Amendment, promised equal rights to all citizens of the United States, especially to the freed slaves. Yet 100 years later, it was still very difficult to be black in America.

Dr. King pointed out that the U.S. government had not kept its promises. Blacks and whites were not treated equally. Southern states had laws separating blacks and whites. Such a system is called **segregation.** Signs on restaurants and theaters throughout the South still read "For Whites Only." Blacks and whites could not use the same restrooms. They could not sit together on a bus. Some white people even threatened blacks to keep them from voting or demanding better treatment.

©Flip Schulke/CORBIS

On August 28, 1963, about 250,000 protestors gathered around the Lincoln Memorial during the March on Washington. They came to demand civil rights for all Americans.

The North did not have these strict segregation laws. But conditions for blacks were not much better there. African Americans still did not have the same opportunities as white people. They could not attend the best schools or apply for good jobs. **Discrimination** still existed, and it was just as painful.

Dr. King knew all of this was wrong. He said that the African Americans' struggle was everyone's struggle. He believed that no one could truly be free unless all people were.

The March on Washington shaped American history. It was an important part of the **Civil Rights Movement.** Blacks all over the country were fighting to be treated fairly. Some African Americans fought their battles in courts of law. Others used **direct action.**

One form of direct action was a **sit-in.** During a sit-in, blacks would sit down at a segregated lunch counter and ask to be served. It was a way to **protest** against segregation laws. The restaurant workers usually refused to serve them. But the protestors would wait calmly, for many hours if necessary. Sometimes people were violent toward them. The protesters were often arrested for breaking segregation laws.

Mass meetings were another form of direct action. At these meetings, people came together to give out information or organize a **demonstration.** These meetings also created a sense of unity among civil rights workers when times were hard. People sang **spirituals** and gospel songs. Black preachers usually led these meetings, which were often held in black churches. Demonstrations were also a type of direct action. The March on Washington was a huge demonstration. People came from across the country to show their support for the Civil Rights Movement.

The idea for a demonstration this big was not new. A man named A. Philip Randolph had the idea in 1941. He started the first black **labor union.** It was called the Brotherhood of Sleeping Car Porters. Randolph thought that good jobs were the first step toward black freedom.

©Bettmann/CORBIS

THESE TWO AFRICAN AMERICAN STUDENTS STUDIED WHILE THEY PARTICIPATED IN A SIT-IN. THEY REFUSED TO LEAVE A LUNCH COUNTER THAT WAS RESERVED FOR WHITE CUSTOMERS. SIT-INS WERE ONE WAY IN WHICH PEOPLE PROTESTED SEGREGATION AND DISCRIMINATION DURING THE CIVIL RIGHTS MOVEMENT.

CIVIL RIGHTS LEADER A. PHILIP RANDOLPH FIRST PROPOSED THE MARCH ON WASHINGTON FOR JOBS AND FREEDOM IN 1941. THAT EVENT WAS CANCELED, BUT RANDOLPH PARTICIPATED IN THE 1963 EVENT.

Many new jobs were created for Americans when World War II began. Randolph wanted to make sure that these jobs would be open to blacks. He proposed a March on Washington for Jobs and Freedom. A young man named Bayard Rustin was hired to help him plan it. Their plan convinced President Franklin D. Roosevelt to sign an **executive order** to stop discrimination in defense industries. Randolph hoped this order would make a difference. He canceled the March of 1941.

Unfortunately, things improved only a little. It became clear that blacks needed to work together for civil rights. The oldest civil rights group was the National Association for the Advancement of Colored People (NAACP). It was formed in 1909 and had both black and white members. The NAACP fought for equal rights through the courts. It won many important cases. One of its most important battles was *Brown versus the Topeka Board of Education.* This court case outlawed segregation in schools. As of 1954, it was no longer legal to make blacks and whites go to separate schools.

Other civil rights groups believed there was strength in numbers. They organized large demonstrations to call attention to the unfair treatment of blacks. In the early 1940s, the Congress of Racial Equality (CORE) held demonstrations in Chicago. It organized sit-ins in restaurants that would not serve African Americans. At best, the demonstrators were ignored. At worst, they were beaten, jailed, or both. No matter what happened, they tried to sit there calmly. Sit-ins became a key tactic in the struggle for civil rights.

Boycotts were another important strategy. The Montgomery bus boycott helped end segregation on public buses. Blacks in Montgomery, Alabama, did not ride the city buses for 381 days. They did this to protest the arrest of Rosa Parks. The city had laws that required African Americans to give up their seats if white people boarded the bus. On December 1, 1955, Mrs. Parks refused to give up her seat for a white man. She was arrested and put in jail for breaking the law.

©Bettmann/CORBIS

ONE OF THE MOST FAMOUS PROTESTS DURING THE CIVIL RIGHTS
MOVEMENT WAS THE MONTGOMERY BUS BOYCOTT. IT HELPED
CHANGE THE LAWS SEPARATING BLACKS AND WHITES ON BUSES. AT
THE END OF THE BOYCOTT, BLACK PASSENGERS ON MONTGOMERY'S
BUSES COULD SIT WHEREVER THEY PLEASED.

The Montgomery bus boycott was important for many reasons. Mrs. Parks showed that the action of one person could make a difference. The boycott proved that blacks could win if they worked together. In December of 1956, the Supreme Court ruled that bus segregation was illegal.

The bus boycott was important for another reason, too. The Montgomery Improvement Association was formed to organize and carry out the boycott. A young black preacher who had just moved to Montgomery was chosen to be its president. His name was Martin Luther King, Jr.

©Bettmann/CORBIS

DR. KING (CENTER) LED THE BOYCOTT OF MONTGOMERY'S BUSES. HE AND MANY OTHER PROTESTORS WERE ARRESTED FOR PARTICIPATING IN THE BOYCOTT.

We've Come Here Today

When people think of the March on Washington, they usually think of the speech made by Dr. Martin Luther King. It is known by one of its key phrases, "I Have a Dream." Dr. King spoke at the end of the day. His speech touched the hearts of all who had come to Washington to march for freedom.

But the march was more than just Dr. King's speech. It was the result of the hard work of many people. More than 250,000 people came to the march. They traveled by bus, car, and airplane. One group walked all the way from Brooklyn, New York. One 82-year-old man rode a bicycle from Dayton, Ohio. One person even came all the way from Chicago on roller skates!

All the major civil rights groups came together to support the march. These groups did not always agree on the best way to work for civil rights. The NAACP usually preferred to work through the courts. They liked to be cautious. So did another group, the National Urban League. Groups such as CORE and the Southern Christian Leadership Conference (SCLC) preferred to use direct action. Dr. King created the SCLC after the success of the Montgomery bus boycott. Black ministers led the group. Black churches were always an important part of the Civil Rights Movement.

©CORBIS

MARTIN LUTHER KING'S SPEECH IS THE MOST FAMOUS MOMENT OF THE MARCH ON WASHINGTON, BUT HUNDREDS OF PEOPLE WORKED TOGETHER TO MAKE THE DEMONSTRATION HAPPEN.

CIVIL RIGHTS LEADERS AT THE MARCH GATHERED AT THE LINCOLN MEMORIAL FOR A PORTRAIT. LEADERS FROM MANY DIFFERENT GROUPS CAME TOGETHER TO DEMAND EQUAL RIGHTS.

The Student Nonviolent Coordinating Committee (SNCC) was one of the youngest groups involved in the march. Most of its members were college students. Students founded the SNCC in 1960 with the help of Dr. King. This group also used direct action. But the young students became impatient with its slow results. The SNCC wanted to be more aggressive. Unfortunately, being more aggressive often **provoked** a violent response from whites, especially in the South. Some of the older groups did not like the risks that the SNCC took.

Still, the leaders of these groups put aside their differences to support the march. Known as the Big Six, these leaders were A. Philip Randolph and Roy Wilkins of the NAACP, Whitney M. Young, Jr., from the Urban League, James Farmer from CORE, Martin Luther King from the SCLC, and John Lewis from the SNCC. These men devoted their lives to the struggle for black freedom.

The Big Six decided to reach out to white civil rights groups. Many civil rights leaders were also religious leaders. They shared a common faith in God. They also valued brotherhood and equality. The white leaders included one Catholic, one Protestant, and one Jew. There was also the leader of a large labor union, the United Auto Workers. These leaders were known as the Top Ten.

Bayard Rustin was the deputy director of the march. He was not one of the Big Six or the Top Ten. His role was behind the scenes. Rustin had been involved in the struggle for civil rights all his life. As a young student, he helped Randolph with the Brotherhood of Sleeping Car Porters. He also worked with CORE and the SCLC in many important **campaigns** that organized people to fight for civil rights.

If King was the march's public face, Rustin was its private one. He only had two months to plan all the details. He worked on transportation, parking, security, food, medical care, and even cleanup. Rustin believed that thinking of people's needs was the key to a smooth event. He tried to think of everything.

Rustin convinced the telephone company to install hundreds of pay phones for free. This helped the organizers stay in touch with each other. He asked the army to donate 40,000 blankets. Volunteers in Harlem made 80,000 bag lunches. Workers set up several thousand portable toilets and 24 first-aid stations along the march route.

Many famous people came to show their support. African American celebrities Sidney Poitier, Lena Horne, Mahalia Jackson, and Harry Belafonte were all at the march. Author James Baldwin and dancer Josephine Baker were there, too. Many of these celebrities entertained the marchers. There were also performances by folk singers Joan Baez, Bob Dylan, and the trio Peter, Paul, and Mary. Actors Marlon Brando and Charlton Heston were also there.

The marchers were instructed to gather at the Washington Monument. During this time, the leaders met with members of congress and other government officials. They planned to join the crowd after these meetings. They would then lead the march down the **Mall** to the Lincoln Memorial. That was where the main program would take place.

Organizers hoped that 100,000 people would come to the march. But there were already 100,000 by 11:00 AM. And more were coming! All roads and highways leading to the capital city were jammed with people. They were tired from their long journeys, but their spirits were high. There was an electric energy in the air. The marchers were united in the spirit of justice and equality.

VOLUNTEERS IN NEW YORK CITY PACKED LUNCHES FOR PROTESTORS
WHO WERE HEADING TO THE MARCH ON WASHINGTON. THE MARCH
WAS THE RESULT OF HARD WORK BY MANY, MANY PEOPLE.

©Bettmann/CORBIS

DEMONSTRATORS MARCHED DOWN THE MALL, FROM THE WASHINGTON MONUMENT TO THE LINCOLN MEMORIAL, CARRYING SIGNS DEMANDING BETTER JOBS, NON-SEGREGATED SCHOOLS, AND CIVIL RIGHTS.

The Struggle for Freedom

The March on Washington was a celebration of freedom. It brought people together in the struggle for civil rights. The path from the Washington Monument to the Lincoln Memorial was two miles long. It was strewn with promise. Many of the marchers walked arm in arm. It felt good just to be there.

The victories of the past had not come easily. Many civil rights workers had been jailed, beaten, and even killed. But they were willing to take these risks. They believed deeply in **nonviolence,** achieving a goal without hurting others. They learned how to cope with insults. They even learned how to protect themselves while being beaten.

A few months earlier, 2,500 people were jailed in Birmingham, Alabama. At least 2,000 were school-age children. They were put in jail because they demonstrated for civil rights. Many of the children were attacked by police dogs. They were sprayed with fire hoses. The force of the water was enough to take the bark off a tree. Even then the protestors did not use violence.

The Birmingham campaign was a dramatic example of the use of direct action. Even Dr. King went to jail for eight days. While he was in jail, he wrote a letter about the use of nonviolence. Dr. King knew that demonstrations caused tension. He explained that this tension was necessary to uncover the deep roots of **racism.** Civil rights workers learned to take beatings and go to jail peacefully. Then the violent actions of others could not be ignored.

Unfortunately, some people simply could not bear the injustice of segregation. Violence exploded after Dr. King left Birmingham. It spread to other cities across the United States.

PROTESTS THAT USED DIRECT ACTION SOMETIMES BECAME VIOLENT, ESPECIALLY IN THE SOUTH. IN MAY OF 1963, POLICE SPRAYED FIRE HOSES AT PROTESTORS DURING A DEMONSTRATION IN BIRMINGHAM, ALABAMA. THIS EVENT TOOK PLACE ABOUT FOUR MONTHS BEFORE THE MARCH ON WASHINGTON.

On June 19, 1963, President John F. Kennedy introduced a new civil rights bill. It put the power of the federal government on the side of equal rights. Black men had won the right to vote in 1870. (Women of any race could not vote until 1920.) But some white people found ways to stop them. Various types of segregation had been outlawed many times, yet discrimination and segregation still continued. People simply ignored these civil rights laws.

Kennedy's new bill said that federal money would not be given to states that ignored civil rights laws. President Kennedy knew that civil rights groups were planning the March on Washington. He was afraid the march might become violent. Kennedy did not think the marchers would become violent, but he was afraid that **hate groups,** such as the Ku Klux Klan, would. He hoped this bill would stop the march the way Roosevelt's bill had stopped the march of 1941. But history did not repeat itself.

The march organizers knew that it would be hard to convince Congress to vote for the bill. Many people, especially in the SNCC, did not think this bill was strong enough. But it was all they had. Organizers decided that the March on Washington should become a loud message to Congress. It should tell government leaders to pass this civil rights bill now!

On the day of the march, a formal program at the Lincoln Memorial began at 1 PM. Each of the Top Ten leaders gave a speech. There were other events as well. Gospel singer Mahalia Jackson sang. There was a tribute to "Negro Women Fighters for Freedom," led by Myrlie Evers. Her husband, Medgar Evers, was an active NAACP leader in Mississippi. He had been shot and killed two months earlier outside of his home.

Everyone knew the highlight of the day would be the speech by Dr. King. He was famous for giving great speeches. None of the other speakers wanted to talk after he did. So Dr. King was scheduled to speak at the end of the program.

©Flip Schulke/CORBIS

CIVIL RIGHTS LEADERS, INCLUDING DR. KING (SECOND FROM LEFT), MET WITH PRESIDENT KENNEDY AND VICE PRESIDENT JOHNSON BEFORE THE MARCH. KENNEDY WORRIED THAT THE MARCH MIGHT BECOME VIOLENT. HE INTRODUCED A BILL THAT HE HOPED WOULD STOP THE MARCH, BUT IT DID NOT.

Martin King was a natural-born speaker. As a child, he loved to learn and use new words. The bigger the word, the better. He had a deep, powerful voice. In the 11th grade, Martin won a prize for giving a speech called "The Negro and the Constitution." This prize had a bitter aftertaste, however. Martin had traveled to the speech contest by bus. On the way home, he was forced to give up his seat to a white person. He was angry all the way home. The injustice of segregation had made its mark on the young man.

Martin grew up in Atlanta in the 1930s and 1940s. His family was more **privileged** than many black families of the time. His father was the well-loved pastor of a thriving church. His mother, too, was highly respected and an important part of the parish. Martin grew up with the church at the center of his world. He considered other careers, but it was not surprising that he eventually decided to become a pastor.

Martin had a bright, gifted mind. He graduated from Morehouse College. The president of Morehouse, Dr. Benjamin Mays, became a close advisor and friend. Dr. Mays gave the closing blessing after King's "I Have a Dream" speech.

Martin next went to Crozer Theological Seminary. (A theological seminary is a school where people study religion.) It was there that his gift for **oratory,** or speech making, blossomed. He studied the craft of preaching with zeal, and he excelled at it. King's practice **sermons** were always crowded with his friends and fellow students.

Crozer introduced Martin to many new subjects. He studied the **Social Gospel Movement.** This movement taught preachers how to use their positions to make changes in the world as well as to give people spiritual guidance. Before this movement, it was more common for preachers to say that freedom and justice happened in heaven. Oppressed people were told to wait for freedom from God. The Social Gospel Movement said that they could instead fight for freedom on Earth.

King also learned about a man named Mahatma Gandhi (pronounced ma-HUT-ma GAHN-dee). Gandhi used direct action and nonviolence to free India from British rule. King had deep respect for Gandhi. He used many of his teachings to develop civil rights actions.

Martin King wanted to get as much education as possible. His father, Reverend Martin Luther King, Sr., wanted his son to work with him at his church in Atlanta. But Martin Jr. wanted to learn even more. After Crozer, he went to Boston University to earn his **doctorate.** He met his wife, Coretta, in Boston. After they finished school, the couple moved to Montgomery, Alabama, in 1954. Martin became the pastor of the Dexter Avenue Baptist Church. Now people called him *Dr.* King, in honor of the degree he had earned at school.

The Dexter ministry called upon all of Dr. King's skills and training. He was a learned **theologian.** He was an electrifying preacher. Most of all, he was a loving and kind pastor. He showed a personal interest in all of the members of his church. He cared deeply about them and their lives. And they cared deeply about him.

Dr. King was an extremely gifted man. His leadership during the Montgomery bus boycott made the boycott work. He was a shining star in a long tradition of black preachers. Many other black preachers also worked for civil rights with their churches. Black churches were the heart and soul of the movement.

©Bettmann/CORBIS

MAHATMA GANDHI WAS A HINDU LEADER WHO USED
DIRECT ACTION TO FREE INDIA FROM BRITISH RULE.
HE USED NONVIOLENCE, A WAY OF PROTESTING
WITHOUT HURTING OTHERS. MARTIN LUTHER KING,
JR., GREATLY ADMIRED GANDHI. KING USED MANY
OF THE SAME FORMS OF PROTEST THAT GANDHI
USED. BOTH MEN BELIEVED THAT VIOLENT OR ANGRY
ACTIONS COULD BE STOPPED WHEN NO VIOLENCE OR
ANGER WAS SHOWN IN RETURN.

Express Photos/Archive Photos

MANY PEOPLE IN THE CROWD BEGAN TO SHOUT "HALLELUJAH!" AND "YES, DOCTOR!" AS MARTIN LUTHER KING SPOKE. THIS TYPE OF RESPONSE IS CUSTOMARY IN MANY BLACK CHURCHES. BUT DR. KING MADE IT CLEAR THAT HE SPOKE NOT ONLY TO BLACKS. HE CALLED OUT TO "ALL GOD'S CHILDREN," BLACK AND WHITE. HE WANTED FREEDOM AND JUSTICE FOR ALL.

Dignity and Discipline

In 1963, Dr. King was the pastor of the Ebeneezer Baptist Church in Atlanta, Georgia. He also traveled all over the United States talking about freedom and justice. Even though he was a famous person, he still cared about the people who belonged to his church. They were all important to him. He knew how many children they had and what their names were. He knew what they did for a living. He knew what they cared about.

It would be impossible for anyone to know the names of all the people who came to the March on Washington. But Dr. King was their pastor, too. He cared as deeply about them as he did about the people in his own church. Dr. King was like a pastor to the entire country. A. Philip Randolph introduced him as, "the **moral** leader of our nation."

Dr. King was also a very educated person. He studied many different subjects. History, philosophy, and religion were among his favorites. When he wrote a speech, he always considered what great thinkers before him had said. In the speech he wrote for the march, he remembered America's founders and Abraham Lincoln. Those American leaders also cared about freedom.

Dr. King worked on his speech late into the night before the march. The speech he wrote called up the promises of the Declaration of Independence, the Constitution, and the Emancipation Proclamation. It told how America had not lived up to the ideal of democracy.

This speech is famous for the words, "I Have a Dream." But the first half of Dr. King's speech told of a nightmare. It told of the African American struggle since the end of slavery. Almost 100 years after Lincoln ended slavery, blacks were not yet truly free. Dr. King spoke of the poverty blacks still faced. He spoke of the poor quality of the neighborhoods in which they lived. He spoke of the discrimination they still experienced.

"**B**ut one hundred years later," proclaimed Dr. King, "the Negro still is not free; one hundred years later, the life of the Negro is still sadly crippled by the **manacles** of segregation and the chains of discrimination; one hundred years later, the Negro lives on a lonely island of poverty in the midst of material prosperity; one hundred years later, the Negro is still languished in the corners of American society and finds himself in exile in his own land."

The deep, powerful voice of Dr. King told a somber story. As he spoke, he looked out into the crowd. So many had come from so far away. They were listening to him carefully. It was as though their hearts were joined.

Dr. King was near the end of the speech he had prepared. Looking out into the crowd, he remembered another speech he had given in Detroit. Even though he had been speaking of a nightmare, suddenly he remembered a dream.

When Dr. King said the words, "I *still* have a dream . . . ," he left his prepared speech behind. He spoke from his heart of his hope for America. Dr. King dared to dream of equality and freedom for all.

His deep patriotism shone through as well. Dr. King recited the words of "My County 'Tis of Thee." Every American knows that song. "Let freedom ring!" he cried. "Let freedom ring!"

Dr. King spoke not only with his voice. His arms stretched out to his audience. The spirit of his words lifted him off his heels. His whole body was filled with the courage and **conviction** of his truth.

Dr. King ended his speech with the words of an African American spiritual. Slaves sang these songs to lift their spirits in the worst times. They used them as a way to remember the African cultures from which they came. In the same way, Dr. King offered this song as a song of hope to all people. "Free at last!" called out Dr. King, "Free at last! Thank God Almighty, we are free at last."

©Flip Schulke/CORBIS

"I HAVE A DREAM," PROCLAIMED DR. KING, "MY FOUR LITTLE CHILDREN WILL ONE DAY LIVE IN A NATION WHERE THEY WILL NOT BE JUDGED BY THE COLOR OF THEIR SKIN BUT BY THE CONTENT OF THEIR CHARACTER. I HAVE A DREAM TODAY!"

©Hulton-Deutsch Collection/ORBIS

CORETTA SCOTT KING ONCE SAID OF THE MARCH THAT "IT SEEMED AS
THOUGH THE KINGDOM OF GOD HAD DESCENDED, BUT IT WAS NOT TO
LAST." THE SPIRIT OF THE MARCH FILLED ITS PARTICIPANTS WITH HOPE
AND OPTIMISM, BUT THERE WOULD BE DIFFICULT TIMES AHEAD.

Free at Last

ans saw
mous speech.
vered the
ndreds of
writers at the
erica, a U.S.
asts in other
name. It
of the day all

ng. There
pport in other
France, and
ugust 28.
al demonstration
ana. This African
ome of W. E. B.
unders of the
is died the day

like this was a new
sion, people had to
newspapers for
more difficult to
pening far away.

de,

Television helped the Civil Rights Movement tell its story. People could actually see for themselves what was happening. They could see the police in Birmingham turn their fire hoses on children. They could see groups of civil rights workers being sent to jail. It was difficult to turn away from such brutal images.

The power of Dr. King's speech also came through on television. More people saw him that day than could fit into any church. Dr. King traveled a lot. He went all over the world. But he could never have spoken to as many people as he did that day. Television made it possible.

The March on Washington was a great success. The marchers behaved with dignity and respect. There was no violence. Everyone left the Lincoln Memorial peacefully when the day was over. Crews cleaned up any litter on the Mall. Cars, buses, and trains carried the tired marchers back to their homes.

Everyone felt proud of what had happened. They had stood together for their beliefs. The marchers showed the world that Americans still cared about freedom. Most important, they showed that Americans cared about each other. Dr. King's speech put people's feelings into words.

Unfortunately, this good will soon passed. On September 15, less than one month later, a bomb exploded in a church in Birmingham. Four young girls were killed in the basement restroom. Most people believed that a white hate group planted the bomb. The killers were never convicted.

More violent acts broke out across the nation. On November 22, President Kennedy was killed in Dallas, Texas. Lyndon Johnson became president. On July 2, 1964, he signed the civil rights bill for which Kennedy had worked. That was almost one year after the march.

Our nation was also at war in Vietnam. Many people thought this war was wrong. So did Dr. King. He said that civil rights were human rights, and that they included the people in faraway Vietnam. All people were brothers and sisters, he said. African Americans were not alone in their struggle. It was the struggle of **oppressed** people everywhere.

Dr. King wanted to have another march on Washington. He planned to call this one "The Poor People's Campaign." It was scheduled for April of 1968. But Dr. King would not be able to lead this march. On April 4, 1968, he was **assassinated** in Memphis, Tennessee.

Dr. King was one of the greatest leaders of our time. He had a brilliant mind and a compassionate heart. He had the courage to dream of a just world, to dream of a country where all citizens were treated with dignity. His greatness reached out to touch the hearts of ordinary people. It continues to inspire each of us to find our own compassion within.

Archive Photos

ONE YEAR AFTER THE MARCH ON WASHINGTON, THE NEW PRESIDENT, LYNDON B. JOHNSON, SIGNED THE CIVIL RIGHTS BILL FOR WHICH PRESIDENT KENNEDY HAD WORKED. MARTIN LUTHER KING WAS THERE TO PARTICIPATE IN THE HISTORIC EVENT.

Timeline

1865	Congress enacts the 13th Amendment, making slavery illegal in the United States.
1868	The 14th Amendment promises civil rights to all Americans.
1870	The 15th Amendment gives men of all races the right to vote.
1909	The National Association for the Advancement of Colored People is founded.
1911	The National Urban League is founded.
1941	A. Philip Randolph proposes what he calls a "March on Washington for Jobs and Freedom." The march is canceled when President Roosevelt signs an executive order prohibiting discrimination in the defense industry.
1942	The Congress of Racial Equality is founded.
1948	Martin Luther King, Jr., graduates from Morehouse College at age 15.
1951	King graduates from Crozer Theological Seminary and is ordained as a Baptist minister.
1954	The Supreme Court outlaws school segregation.
1955	King receives a doctorate in theology from Boston University.
	On December 1, Rosa Parks refuses to give up her bus seat to a white man. She is arrested for violating segregation laws. The Montgomery bus boycott begins. Dr. King leads the boycott.
1956	The Montgomery bus boycott continues for more than a year before the Supreme Court rules that the buses cannot be segregated.
1957	Dr. King founds the Southern Christian Leadership Conference.
1960	The Student Nonviolent Coordinating Committee is founded.
1963	On May 2, African American children and young people gather for a demonstration in Birmingham, Alabama. More than 900 are arrested. The next day, thousands more children gather to protest. The police use dogs and fire hoses to stop them and arrest more than 2,500 protestors, mostly children. The violence of the police is shown on television, angering people around the country.
	On June 19, President Kennedy introduces a new civil rights bill.
	On August 28, about 250,000 people participate in the March on Washington for Jobs and Freedom. The highlight of the march is Dr. King's speech.
1964	President Lyndon Johnson signs Kennedy's civil rights bill into law on July 2. Dr. King is present for the event.
1968	Dr. King announces plans for a Poor People's Campaign on Washington.
	On April 4, Dr. King is assassinated in Memphis, Tennessee.

Glossary

assassinated (uh-SASS-ih-nay-ted)
When well-known people are murdered, we say assassinated. Martin Luther King, Jr. was assassinated.

boycotts (BOY-kots)
Boycotts are protests in which people stop using a certain product or service. Boycotts were used frequently throughout the Civil Rights Movement.

campaigns (kam-PAYNZ)
During the Civil Rights Movement, campaigns were when groups (such as the SCLC) traveled to a town to help people fight for equal rights. The national groups provided leadership and guidance to local people.

Civil Rights Movement (SIV-el RYTZ MOOV-mint)
The Civil Rights Movement was the African American struggle for equal rights that took place during the 1950s and 1960s. Martin Luther King, Jr., was a leader of the Civil Rights Movement.

conviction (kun-VIK-shun)
A conviction is a strong belief. Dr. King had strong convictions about equal rights.

demonstration (dem-un-STRAY-shun)
A demonstration is a gathering of people who want to show their support for a cause. The March on Washington was one of the biggest demonstrations in American history.

direct action (dih-REKT AK-shen)
Direct action is any form of protest that publicly shows a group's views. Marches, boycotts, and sit-ins were direct actions used in the Civil Rights Movement.

discrimination (dis-krim-ih-NAY-shun)
Discrimination is the unfair treatment of people simply because they are different. African Americans have suffered discrimination by whites.

doctorate (DOK-ter-ut)
A doctorate is an advanced degree from a college or university. Martin Luther King, Jr., received his doctorate from Boston University.

executive order (eg-ZEK-yew-tiv OR-der)
An executive order is a rule made by the president or other leader that has the power of a law. President Roosevelt signed an executive order to end discrimination in the defense industry.

hate groups (HAYT GROOPZ)
Hate groups are clubs or organizations whose members share a common hatred for other races, religions, or other people with differences. The Ku Klux Klan is a hate group.

labor union (LAY-bor YOO-nyen)
A labor union is a group of workers who join together to protect their interests. Labor unions make sure that their members earn fair wages and are treated well.

Mall (MAWL)
The Mall in Washington, D.C., is a wide, grassy public walking area that is more than two miles long. It stretches from the U.S. Capitol to the Lincoln Memorial.

manacles (MAN-uh-kulz)
Manacles are chains used like handcuffs to keep people from moving their hands. Martin Luther King, Jr. said that the "manacles of segregation" ruined the lives of African Americans.

Glossary

moral (MOR-ul)
If people are moral, they are good or just. Moral people know the difference between right and wrong.

nonviolence (non-VY-oh-lence)
Nonviolence is the belief that people can demonstrate for change without hurting others. Civil rights workers were trained in nonviolence and learned not to respond with anger when people showed anger toward them.

oppressed (oh-PREST)
If people are oppressed, they are treated unfairly or cruelly. Martin Luther King, Jr., wanted to help oppressed people everywhere, not just African Americans.

oratory (OR-uh-tor-ee)
Oratory is the art of public speaking. Martin Luther King, Jr., was a great public speaker and orator.

privileged (PRIV-ih-lejd)
If people are privileged, they have special advantages that other people do not. When he was a child, Dr. King's family was more privileged than other black families.

protest (PRO-test)
If people protest against something, they speak out to say that it is wrong. Americans of all races joined the 1963 March on Washington to protest the treatment of blacks.

provoke (pruh-VOHK)
If people provoke others, they make them angry or cause them to react in some way. Martin Luther King, Jr., believed that if protestors used violence, it provoked more violence from others.

racism (RAY-sih-zim)
Racism is a negative feeling or opinion about people because of their race. Racism can be committed by individuals, large groups, or even governments.

segregation (seh-greh-GAY-shun)
Segregation is a situation in which actions and laws separate people from one another. Segregation laws kept blacks and whites apart in the South for many years.

sermons (SUR-munz)
Sermons are public talks related to religion, usually given by a religious leader. Martin Luther King, Jr., was well known for his moving sermons.

sit-in (SIT-in)
A sit-in was a form of direct action during the civil rights movement. Sit-ins were often held at restaurants that would not serve blacks.

Social Gospel Movement (SO-shul GOS-pell MOOV-mint)
The Social Gospel Movement encouraged preachers to use their churches as places to talk about civil rights. Black churches were important centers of the Civil Rights Movement.

spirituals (SPEER-ih-chewls)
Spirituals are religious songs based on stories or events from the Bible. They were created and sung by African Americans, especially during the time of slavery.

theologian (thee-oh-LOW-jen)
A theologian is a person who studies religious beliefs and the history of religion. Martin Luther King, Jr. was a theologian.

Index

Further Information

Books

Andryszewski,Tricia. *The March on Washington, 1963: Gathering to Be Heard.*
Brookfield, CT: Millbrook Press, 1996.

Haskins, Jim. *I Have a Dream: The Life and Words of Martin Luther King, Jr.*
Brookfield, CT: Millbrook Press, 1992.

Haskins, James, with introduction by James Farmer. *The March on Washington.*
New York: HarperCollins, 1993.

King, Martin Luther, Jr. *I Have a Dream* (with a foreword by Reverend Bernice A. King,
Dr. King's daughter). San Francisco: Harper San Francisco, 1993.

Siegel, Beatrice. *The Year They Walked: Rosa Parks and the Montgomery Bus Boycott.*
New York: Simon & Schuster, 1992.

Web Sites

Read the entire "I Have a Dream" speech:
http://web66.coled.umn.edu/new/MLK/MLK.htm

Access an African American history Web site:
http://www.triadntr.net/~rdavis/

Lists and links for many interesting sites about Martin Luther King, including articles,
photographs, quotes, a free coloring book, quizzes, and more:
http://martinlutherking.8m.com/

Video

See Martin Luther King, Jr., give his most famous speech:
Martin Luther King, Jr. — "I Have a Dream." MPI Home Video (1986).

Watch a biography of Martin Luther King, Jr.:
Biography: Martin Luther King, Jr. A&E Home Video (1997).